CULTURE IN ACTION

Destroy After Reading

THE WORLD OF SECRET CODES

Mary Colson

Raintree

Chicago, Illinois

www.heinemannraintree.com

Visit our website to find out more information about Heinemann-Raintree books.

To order:

☎ Phone 888-454-2279

🖥 Visit www.heinemannraintree.com to browse our catalog and order online.

Edited by Louise Galpine and Diyan Leake
Designed by Victoria Allen
Original illustrations © Capstone Global Library Ltd 2011
Illustrated by Randy Schirz
Picture research by Hannah Taylor

Originated by Capstone Global Library Ltd
Printed in and bound in China by CTPS

14 13 12 11 10
10 9 8 7 6 5 4 3 2 1

Library of Congress Cataloging-in-Publication Data
Colson, Mary.
 Destroy after reading : the world of secret codes / Mary Colson.
     p. cm. -- (Culture in action)
 Includes bibliographical references and index.
 ISBN 978-1-4109-3927-2
 1. Cryptography--Juvenile literature. 2. Ciphers--Juvenile literature. 3. Cryptography--History--Juvenile literature. 4. Ciphers--History--Juvenile literature. I. Title.
 Z103.3.C65 2011
 652'.8--dc22
                        2009052597

Acknowledgments
The author and publishers are grateful to the following for permission to reproduce copyright material: © Adrian Gaut/Art + Commerce p. **27**; akg-images p. **15** (ullstein bild); Corbis pp. **6** (Bettmann), **8** (Bettmann), **10** (Bettmann), **17** (Bettmann), **23** (Kim Kulish); FBI p. **7** insets; Getty Images pp. **7** main (Keystone), **16** (SSPL); Lebrecht Music & Arts p. **20** main (Arthur Reynolds Collection); Photolibrary pp. **5** (Corbis), **13** (JTB Photo), **18** (Nativestock Pictures), **24** (Robert Llewellyn), **25** (Juice Images), **26** (Kurt Scholz), **28** (Flight Images Llp); Rex Features pp. **14** (Jonathan Hordle), **29**; The National Archives p. **12**; Topfoto p. **4** (The Granger Collection).

Cover photograph of a former Bombe operator with a British Turing Bombe in Bletchley Park Museum, Buckinghamshire, England, September 6, 2006, reproduced with permission of Reuters (Alessia Pierdomenico).

We would like to thank Jackie Murphy for her invaluable help in the preparation of this book.

Every effort has been made to contact copyright holders of any material reproduced in this book. Any omissions will be rectified in subsequent printings if notice is given to the publisher.

Disclaimer
All the Internet addresses (URLs) given in this book were valid at the time of going to press. However, due to the dynamic nature of the Internet, some addresses may have changed, or sites may have changed or ceased to exist since publication. While the author and publisher regret any inconvenience this may cause readers, no responsibility for any such changes can be accepted by either the author or the publisher.

Author

Mary Colson is an experienced teacher and writer of non-fiction books. She is hoping to crack the Beale Ciphers and find the buried treasure!

Literacy consultant

Jackie Murphy is Director of Arts at the Center of Teaching and Learning, Northeastern Illinois University. She works with teachers, artists, and school leaders internationally.

Contents

Some words are printed in bold, **like this**. You can find out what they mean by looking in the glossary on page 30.

What's So Special About Secret Codes?

Secret codes are powerful ways of sending messages and keeping information hidden. Cracking a code is about being a detective and **outwitting** your opponents. Creating, carrying, and cracking codes can be exciting and dangerous, and can even save lives.

Codes have brought down **monarchs** and whole armies and, today, they can make computers work or cause them to crash. Using a code makes sure that messages are understood only by the people they are intended for—from soldiers to **popes**. Some codes are written in letters, some in numbers, some in symbols, and some are only spoken or appear in music. Codes can also be found in pictures, in smoke, and even in string.

The Incas of South America used *quipu*, or "talking knots," to pass information to each other. The *quipu* was a group of colored knotted strings made from llama hair.

A very old art

Codes have been used since ancient times. The word *cryptography* means the "science of codes." It comes from the Greek words *kryptos* (secret) and *graphos* (writing). **Cryptographers** make and break codes. Many modern cryptographers use computer languages or codes to help them **encrypt** and **decrypt** their messages.

The sign of the fish

In ancient Rome, Christians were **persecuted** for their beliefs and forced to hide in underground burial tunnels. They drew a fish on the wall to mark a place to meet. Other Christians would mark the eye of the fish as a code to say they were friends and not enemies.

When you use a computer and send emails, you are using codes that change into a form you can understand.

Early Codes

Hiding a message is the earliest form of code and it is called steganography. In the 400s BCE, a man named Demaratus wrote an urgent message on a **tablet** and then covered it with wax. He sent the tablet to some Greek friends, who removed the wax and saw the hidden writing telling them the Persian army was going to invade!

Around 2,000 years ago, the Chinese wrote secret messages on hard-boiled eggs. "Invisible" ink sank into the shell, and the message was revealed on the hard white of the egg once the shell was removed.

Secret tattoos

In ancient Greece, messages were even tattooed on shaved heads! Once the hair had grown back, the servant would deliver the message, which would be revealed by shaving the head again!

Shining a special light on a letter written in invisible ink will let the secret message show through.

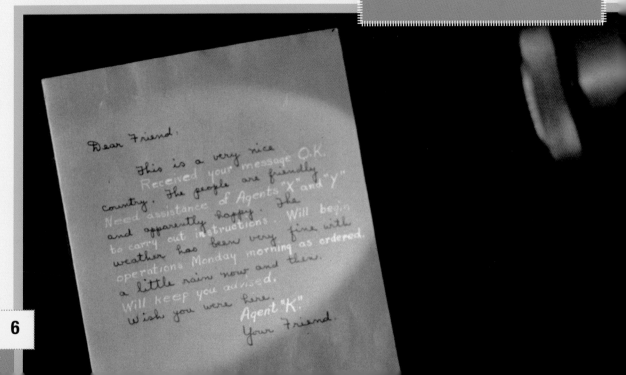

"Doll in a hula skirt"

Secret messages were still being used in the 1900s. In 1941 the Japanese unexpectedly bombed the U.S. naval base at Pearl Harbor in Hawaii, killing many U.S. service people and damaging many ships. A spy for the Japanese named Velvalee Dickinson owned a doll store in New York City. She used doll orders to send messages back to the Japanese. She once wrote: "Doll in a hula skirt is in the hospital and doctors are working around the clock." This really meant: "USS *Honolulu* is badly damaged and undergoing around-the-clock repairs." Dickinson was eventually caught and **convicted** of espionage (spying) against the United States.

The USS *Shaw* had been damaged in the Japanese attack on Pearl Harbor. The spy Velvalee Dickinson reported on this in a letter, calling the ship "Mr. Shaw."

You wrote me that you had sent a letter to
xxx Mr.Shaw,well I went to see MR.CHAW
he distroyed YOUR letter,you know he has
been ILL. His car was damaged but
is being repaired now.I saw a few of his
family about.They all say Mr.Shaw will be
back to work soon..

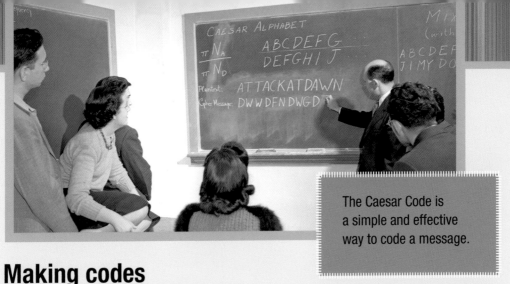

Making codes

Throughout history, people have wanted to keep their messages secret. But hidden writing is risky, because once the messenger or device is searched, the message is revealed easily. Codes are more secure. A code is a system of symbols, letters, words, or signals that are used instead of ordinary words and numbers to send secret messages or store information.

A code fit for an emperor

An early example of a code is the one used by Roman Emperor Julius Caesar. In the Caesar Code, one letter of the alphabet is exchanged for another using a code wheel or grid. This table shows how Caesar wrote his codes.

	A	B	C	D	E	F	G	H	I	J	K	L	M
Caesar Code	X	Y	Z	A	B	C	D	E	F	G	H	I	J
	N	O	P	Q	R	S	T	U	V	W	X	Y	Z
Caesar Code	K	L	M	N	O	P	Q	R	S	T	U	V	W

Using the Caesar Code, figure out the following message:

HBBM VLRO PBZOBQP PXCB!

(The answer is at the bottom of page 9.)

Grid code

A grid code goes one step further than the Caesar Code, changing letters into numbers using the grid on the right. For each letter you take the matching number from the vertical position and then one from the horizontal position. For example, WAR would be 52 11 42. What would PEACE be?

	1	2	3	4	5
1	A	B	C	D	E
2	F	G	H	I or J	K
3	L	M	N	O	P
4	Q	R	S	T	U
5	V	W	X	Y	Z

The Spartan scytale

The scytale (rhymes with "Italy") from Sparta in ancient Greece is an early military code device. Messages were written on a strip of leather (sometimes a servant's belt), which was wrapped around a stick of a certain thickness. The code would only make sense if the receiver of the message wound the belt around a stick of equal thickness.

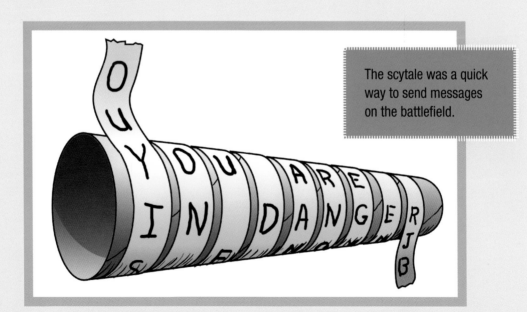

The scytale was a quick way to send messages on the battlefield.

Code Symbols and Cracking Codes

Some codes do not use letters or numbers but rather use drums, flames, or even smoke.

Smoke signals

Smoke signals were used by Native Americans to send information across large distances. Each tribe made its own code by fanning the smoke into the air at different intervals.

Smoke signals are still used today. When a new **pope** is chosen in Rome, church leaders have a secret **ballot**. The results are sent to people waiting outside using smoke signals. Black smoke means they have not decided, and white smoke means a new pope has been elected.

Native Americans made smoke signals to tell others that enemies were near.

Beacon code

In 1588 news of a Spanish invasion was sent to Queen Elizabeth I in London, England, by a chain of hilltop fires called beacons. Beacons were warning fires. When one fire could be seen, the next one was lit.

Send a musical message

In the Civil War in the United States (1861–1865), commanders sent orders to troops and cavalry riders on the battlefield by drum messages and bugle calls. These sounds meant different things, such as "go forward," "retreat," "gallop," or "start firing." You and a friend could imagine that you are spies and create a musical code. You could use bells, whistles, or drums.

Steps to follow:

1. Make up a code with your friend. You could do an alphabet code, so that one sound is A, two are B, and so on, or you could use different sounds for different words. Don't forget that you can use volume and **pitch** as part of your code.

2. Decide on a short message.

3. Practice your code inside and outside your house.

4. Can you and your friend understand each other's message?

11

The importance of a code book

When you replace words, phrases, or sentences with groups of letters, numbers, or symbols, you are making a code. Changing messages into code is called encryption. Having your code cracked can be deadly …

Off with her head!

In the 1580s, Mary, Queen of Scots, sent coded messages to her supporters who were plotting to murder England's Queen Elizabeth I. The messages fell into the hands of Elizabeth's spy chief, Sir Francis Walsingham. He **deciphered** them and then used Mary's code to send messages to her and entrap her. Mary fell into the trap, was found guilty of **treason**, and beheaded.

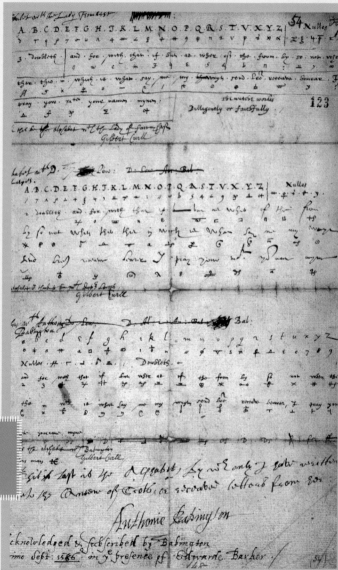

This was the secret code used by Mary, Queen of Scots.

A code stone?

For most codes, there needs to be a codebook in which the meanings of the numbers, symbols, and letters are listed for both the sender and receiver.

Probably the most famous code "book" is actually a stone. For centuries, **archaeologists** puzzled over the strange engravings on Egyptian temples and tombs, known as hieroglyphs. Their meaning was finally deciphered by Jean-François Champollion after the Rosetta Stone was discovered in 1799. The stone has the same text carved in three different scripts, including Greek and hieroglyphics.

The Rosetta Stone is 114.4 centimeters (45 inches) high at its highest point and 72.3 centimeters (28½ inches) wide. It has been exhibited in London's British Museum since 1802.

How to crack a code

Sometimes you can start to crack a code by counting how many times a letter, number, or symbol occurs. You can then compare this to common letters or important names. Both Walsingham and Champollion used this approach. This is how Champollion realized that in hieroglyphics the names of **pharaohs** are always circled.

Code School and the Enigma Machine

In World War II (1939–1945), if employees of the British government's code division got the telephone message "Auntie Flo is not so well," they had to report immediately to Bletchley Park, the government code-cracking headquarters.

Code headquarters

By the early 1940s, Britain was in danger of running out of food. Supply ships from the United States were being sunk by German submarines in the Atlantic Ocean. The British government needed to know the German submarine movements in order to get the supply ships safely into port. To do this, some of the smartest people in the country were hired to work at Bletchley Park. Their job was to crack the thousands of coded messages being sent by the German forces every day.

Bletchley Park was once a family home. The British government chose it as the code-cracking headquarters because of its safe location outside London.

Coding machine

German messages were sent with a machine that looked like an old-fashioned typewriter. This was the Enigma machine. More than just a keyboard, Enigma machines had three wheels with the letters of the alphabet etched around the outside. The wheels were set in a different starting position each morning according to a secret code word. As the operator typed, the wheels turned in different directions and **encrypted** the message.

An impossible puzzle?

Because of all the different possible settings, every time a message was sent to German forces, the Enigma machine could encrypt it in 150 million million million different ways! To crack the Enigma code, the code-breakers needed to know how the wheels had been set to start with. For this, they needed the code book.

This is an Enigma machine. *Enigma* means "puzzle" in Greek.

How was Enigma cracked?

More than 7,000 people worked at Bletchley Park. The code-breakers would analyze and compare the Enigma messages to see if they could figure out how the submarine operators had set their wheels that day. Because the code word changed daily, the code-breakers had to begin the process all over again every 24 hours. With food ships being sunk in the Atlantic Ocean almost daily, it was a race against time to crack the code.

Making a Bombe

Many people worked hard to solve Enigma, from Polish mathematicians to French, British, and U.S. **cryptographers**. At Bletchley Park, Alan Turing created a machine called the Bombe. Bombes "read" hundreds of different Enigma codes a minute and found patterns. Sheila Carman was a Bombe operator. She remembered: "The work went on non-stop so we worked in shifts throughout the day and night, weekends, and public holidays."

Hut 6 was the nerve center of code-cracking at Bletchley Park.

Breakthrough!

Capturing an Enigma code book became essential if the code was going to be cracked. German Navy code books were printed in **water-soluble** ink so that they could be easily destroyed if they were at risk of falling into enemy hands. By 1940 part of the code had been cracked, but in 1944 a code book was captured from the submarine *U-505* and the breakthrough was made.

In cracking the Enigma code, the Bletchley Park code-breakers saved many lives and probably shortened the war. Once the code was cracked, it was kept top secret. The British and the **Allies** could then use the information to their advantage. Like Sir Francis Walsingham, they used an enemy's own code to defeat him.

This is a famous photograph showing the capture of the *U-505* and its crew.

Coding Languages

During World War II, the U.S. military employed over 400 Native Americans to send and receive secret messages over the phone or radio by talking in code. Unlike the Enigma code, the code of the Code Talkers was never broken.

The code was created from various Native American languages. For example, the Navajo word for "potato" was the code word for "bomb" or "grenade." From the Comanche language, a bomber was a "pregnant airplane." A machine gun was a "sewing machine."

Talking numbers

In World War I (1914–1918), radio operators in the trenches were given a code book called *Secret A*. This code book listed all the number codes used to tell commanders far away what was happening at the front line. For example, if a radio operator sent the message "11," it meant the enemy was attacking.

A monument to the Navajo Code Talkers was erected in Arizona.

Using flag code

Hand-held flags are used as a way to send information at airports and on boats. This flag code is called semaphore. The position of the flags represent letters or phrases.

Steps to follow:

1. With a friend, make two flags using pieces of cardboard or cloth and sticks or old rulers.

2. Stand opposite each other and make up a code based on how you each hold your flags. For example, if you hold your flags above your head, it might mean "danger." Flags pointed to the floor might mean "stop."

3. Imagine you are guiding aircraft into position on a runway. One of you should move as if you were the aircraft.

4. Make up a performance routine using your flags.

5. Show your performance to some friends and family. Can they figure out your flag code?

Private codes

Codes can be romantic, too! In England in the 1800s, it was not acceptable for an unmarried man and woman to send each other messages, so lovers sent **encrypted** messages to each other in the personal columns of newspapers. The message would look normal, but the couple would have agreed that every third letter, for example, would spell out a love note.

Composing codes

The composer Edward Elgar loved puzzles and codes. In 1897 he sent a coded letter known as the Dorabella ("Beautiful Dora") **Cipher** to Miss Dora Penny. The problem was, she was unable to **decipher** it, and to this day nobody knows what the letter means! Can you crack the code?

Make your own pinprick encryption

In the early days of the mail service in Great Britain, people paid to receive letters instead of paying to send them. However, it was free to send and receive newspapers. To avoid expense, people used newspapers to send messages. They made tiny pin holes in the newspaper over the tops of letters before mailing them. This was called pinprick encryption.

You and a friend could send your own secret messages!

Steps to follow:

1. Find an old newspaper and a pin.

2. Prick out your secret messages to each other by making pin holes above the letters. For example, you might put a hole above the letters H and I to spell "Hi."

3. When you have finished pricking out your message, swap papers and see if you can decipher each other's message!

TIP: Hold the paper up to the light to see where the holes are.

MANY SECRET MESSAGES ARE VERY TRICKY TO WORK OUT

Computer codes

In the 1820s, the British mathematician Charles Babbage invented a mathematical computer that could be programmed. This was the start of all modern computing.

Today, computers operate all sorts of things, from airplanes to cell phones, televisions, cars, and missiles. But did you know that all computer codes are based around the numbers 0 and 1? Computers only register and understand these two numbers. Computer programs translate all commands into combinations of 0 and 1.

Computer languages

The purpose of computer codes is to make it easy to process and share information. Different coding languages are used for different purposes. COBOL is one of the oldest computer languages. Its name is an **acronym** for **CO**mmon **B**usiness-**O**riented **L**anguage. It is used to operate business and government administrative and finance systems. Java is the code used to operate cell phone applications, Web servers, and Internet browsers.

Computer codes are wherever information is stored or passed on—from banking to the exchange of emails. Codes have long been employed by governments, militaries, businesses, and organizations to protect their electronic messages. Today, stored data and transactions (exchanges in which money is involved) between computers are encrypted to protect them.

Cryptography today

Modern computing encryption developed rapidly during the 1970s. Three important people in this field are Ron Rivest, Adi Shamir, and Leonard Adleman. They developed a system for sending and receiving electronic information that was secure and private. Their code system, called RSA, after the first letters of their last names, means that nobody can read our private emails.

Leonard Adleman, Ron Rivest, and Adi Shamir, (from left to right in the photo) received the A. M. Turing Award in 2002 for inventing the RSA system. The award is given for outstanding contributions in computer science.

Codes of Today and Tomorrow

Today, codes are used in many areas of daily life. They operate home security alarms and make bicycle locks work. Code readers are used in vehicles for quick payment at toll booths on bridges and highways. Code cards are even used in school libraries and cafeterias.

We do not often share codes as we did in the past, but we have personal codes and passwords that we keep secret. There is not usually a need for code books like those of Mary, Queen of Scots, or Enigma, which made their codes **vulnerable**. Now we are all code-makers and code-breakers.

Personal codes

To log on to a computer, you often need a password. This is so only you can access your files and emails. Cell phones can work in this way, too. To get money out of an automated teller machine (ATM), you need a personal identity number (PIN), which only you know.

Bank vaults are protected by complicated security codes.

In baseball, the catcher uses his hands to signal how he or she wants the pitcher to throw the ball. This is a form of code.

Biological codes

Many countries have passports with "biometric" details for security reasons. This means that encoded electronic information about your fingerprints or irises (parts of your eye) is stored.

Sports codes

Codes are used in many sports to keep a team's tactics secret from the opposition. In football, teams have a play book with many different play formations. Team members must learn these "plays," which are usually assigned a number. If the quarterback yells, "16" on the field, then the other players know what the quarterback is going to do with the ball.

Unsolvable codes?

There are some codes that have outfoxed even the best code-breaking minds.

In 1900 large numbers of 3,500-year-old clay **tablets** were discovered on the Mediterranean island of Crete. There were two different types of writing on the tablets. They were named "Linear A" and "Linear B." Linear B was finally **deciphered** in the 1950s by the British **archaeologist** Sir Arthur Evans. Linear A, however, remains unsolved.

Also on Crete, the mysterious Phaistos Disk has still not been deciphered. The 15-centimeter- (6-inch-) wide disk has 45 different symbols and 241 signs stamped into both sides in spiral patterns. There have been lots of suggestions as to the meaning of the code, but no one knows it for sure.

The Phaistos Disk might help to decipher Linear A, the mysterious writing on the clay tablets found on Crete.

Modern mystery

In 1990 a sculpture was installed at the U.S. Central Intelligence Agency (CIA) Headquarters in Langley, Virginia, as a challenge to the agency's employees. The Kryptos sculpture was created by the U.S. sculptor Jim Sanborn. The thousands of characters contain four encrypted messages. So far, three have been solved, but the last message remains a mystery.

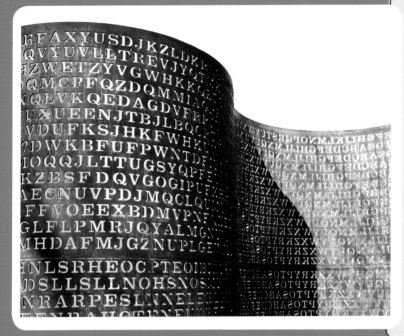

Buried treasure?

Around 1820 a man named Thomas J. Beale is said to have buried nearly 3 tons of treasure at a secret location in Bedford County, Virginia. He then left a small locked box with a local innkeeper and left town, never to be seen or heard of again. After a few years, the innkeeper opened the box and discovered **encrypted** messages. These are known as the Beale **Ciphers**. Only one of the three codes has been deciphered, and the supposed treasure remains unfound.

What we've learned

After thousands of years, our fascination and need for codes is stronger than ever. With progress in computing, medicine, and banking technology, coded passwords and logins are essential to protect information.

Today, people are still trying to figure out the Beale Ciphers and are still trying to crack codes all over the world. Ensuring national security and keeping military secrets means the work of code-makers and code-breakers goes on. Their skills are very valuable, and the work they do is of national and international importance.

The Government Communications Headquarters (GCHQ) building in Cheltenham, England, is nicknamed "the doughnut." GCHQ is the British government's code-cracking headquarters. Workers have to clear their desks and lock everything away in special cabinets every night.

The U.S. National Security Agency (NSA), located in Fort Meade, Maryland, is the world's largest employer of mathematicians.

We have learned that some codes are designed not to be broken and that when we send emails, our words are being encoded for us. We have learned that codes can protect us. We have even learned that codes can save lives.

The future of codes

Whatever the future holds, one thing is certain: from security passwords to PIN numbers and computer logins, we need codes. There are people all over the world making and breaking codes every minute of every day. But who they are and where they work is top secret. They could even be working somewhere near you ...

Celtic Code

Old codes are still being discovered today. In 2009 researchers at Stirling Castle in Scotland deciphered a secret musical code carved into a wooden panel. The code has puzzled people for more than 500 years.

Glossary

acronym word formed from the initials or parts of words

Allies people or countries on the same side in a war. In World War II, the Allies included Great Britain, the United States, and France.

archaeologist person who studies the past by looking at objects that people used to use

ballot election. A ballot is taken to decide issues such as who will become the new president.

cipher secret written code

convicted found guilty of a crime

cryptographer person who writes or figures out the meaning of codes

decipher figure out the meaning of a code

decrypt figure out the meaning of a code

encrypt put plain text into code

monarch king or queen

outwit be smarter or more resourceful than someone else

persecute treat unfairly. People are sometimes persecuted for their religious beliefs or the color of their skin.

pharaoh ruler of ancient Egypt

pitch how high or low a sound is

pope head of the Catholic Church

tablet flat surface of stone or wood with words written on it

treason betrayal of or disloyalty toward your own country

vulnerable weak or fragile

water-soluble can be dissolved in water

Find Out More

Places to visit

National Cryptologic Museum
9800 Savage Road
Fort Meade, Maryland 20755
www.nsa.gov/about/cryptologic_heritage/museum/
This museum of the National Security Agency (NSA) contains thousands of artifacts, including machines and devices, that show the history of making and breaking codes in the United States.

International Spy Museum
800 F Street NW
Washington, D.C. 20004
www.spymuseum.org
This museum has a special "KidSpy" program that allows kids to participate in fun programs such as code-cracking.

Websites

www.nsa.gov/kids/
This website of the NSA features the "CryptoKids" page, where kids can learn how to make and break codes.

https://www.cia.gov/kids-page/index.html
Visit the Central Intelligence Agency (CIA) website to find out the history of the CIA. This page just for kids also includes games.

www.navajocodetalkers.org
Learn more about the Navajo Code Talkers at this website.

Index